ROCKS

GEMSTONES

BY PATRICK PERISH

BELLWETHER MEDIA • MINNEAPOLIS, MN

Blastoff! Discovery launches
a new mission: reading to learn.
Filled with facts and features, each
book offers you an exciting new
world to explore!

This edition first published in 2020 by Bellwether Media, Inc.

No part of this publication may be reproduced in whole or in part
without written permission of the publisher.
For information regarding permission, write to Bellwether Media, Inc.,
Attention: Permissions Department,
6012 Blue Circle Drive, Minnetonka, MN 55343.

Library of Congress Cataloging-in-Publication Data

Names: Perish, Patrick, author.
Title: Gemstones / by Patrick Perish.
Description: Minneapolis, MN : Bellwether Media, Inc., [2020] |
Series: Blastoff! Discovery: Rocks & Minerals |
Audience: Ages 7-13. | Audience: Grades 3 to 8.
Identifiers: LCCN 2019001510 (print) | LCCN 2019003684
   (ebook) | ISBN 9781618916464 (ebook) |
   ISBN 9781644870747 (hardcover : alk. paper) |
   ISBN 9781618917416 (pbk. : alk. paper)
Subjects: LCSH: Gems–Juvenile literature. |
   Precious stones–Juvenile literature.
Classification: LCC QE392.2 (ebook) |
   LCC QE392.2 .P47 2020 (print) | DDC 553.8–dc23
LC record available at https://lccn.loc.gov/2019001510

Editor: Betsy Rathburn   Designer: Jeffrey Kollock

Printed in the United States of America, North Mankato, MN.

TABLE OF CONTENTS

DEVILLINE

PAST AND PRESENT TREASURES

A museum has just acquired a new piece for its collection. It is a necklace studded with blue gemstones. This skillfully crafted work gives museum visitors a glimpse into ancient cultures!

The museum worker carefully handles the necklace. She uses a small brush to remove dust. When she is finished, the worker puts the jewelry away. She removes her gloves and slips on a diamond wedding ring. People have treasured gemstones for thousands of years!

WHAT ARE GEMSTONES?

Gemstones, or gems, are precious objects valued for their appearance. Most gems are **crystals**. Others are brightly colored rocks or **organic** materials. Gems are often cut and **embedded** in jewelry or other items.

Gems have been collected, shaped, and treasured throughout history. They are often used in religious or other special ceremonies. Turquoise is an important stone to Native American tribes of the southwestern United States. This beautiful gem has been used in Native American art for centuries!

AMETHYST CRYSTALS

TURQUOISE
JEWELRY

SERPENTINE

Gems can often be identified by physical properties. Gem hardness is measured using the Mohs scale. Gems are given a rating of 1 to 10. Diamonds are the hardest gemstone. Their Mohs rating is 10!

Luster and color are also important in identifying gems. Metallic gemstones, like pyrite, are shiny. Other gems may be dull, glassy, or greasy. Gems come in all different colors, too. Their colors are determined by the minerals they contain.

GEMSTONE PROFILE

GEMSTONE: **EMERALD**

HARDNESS: 7.5 to 8 on Mohs scale

1 soft	2	3	4	5	6	7	8	9	10 hard

TYPE: crystal gemstone

FOUND: all over the world, with most emeralds mined in Colombia, Zambia, Brazil, and Zimbabwe

MADE OF: a green variety of the mineral beryl

USES: most commonly used in jewelry and other decorative items

9

Gems can be identified by how light passes through them. Transparent gems allow light to pass through easily. Clear diamonds and emeralds are transparent. Translucent gems only allow the glow of light to pass through them. Carnelian is a popular translucent gem. Opaque gems, like jasper, do not allow any light through.

Thickness and shape play a role in how light passes through a gem. The same gems may have different transparencies. Some gems, like agates, can show all three light levels in one stone!

TRANSPARENCY

TRANSPARENT

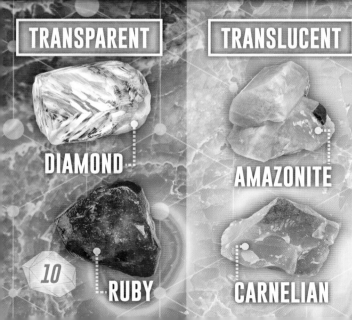

DIAMOND

RUBY

TRANSLUCENT

AMAZONITE

CARNELIAN

OPAQUE

JASPER

PYRITE

BLACK AND GREEN

Black jade is a rare opaque gemstone. When it is held up to light, it looks green!

HOW ARE GEMSTONES MADE?

LAVA

FIND YOUR OWN GEMSTONE

At Crater of Diamonds State Park in Arkansas, visitors can dig for and keep gems. In 1990, a visitor found a 3-carat diamond!

Gemstones form in a few different ways.
When volcanoes erupt, lava flows over Earth's surface.
Then it cools. This process creates crystals! The crystals
look rough at first. People polish and cut the crystals!

Crystals can also form from minerals **dissolved**
in water. The minerals harden. If the conditions are right,
they form crystals! Crystals that grow slowly become the
largest. In time, they may be cut into gemstones!

COMPARING GEMSTONES

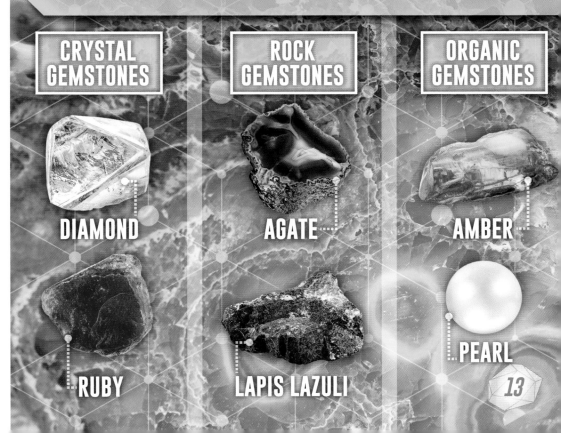

CRYSTAL GEMSTONES	ROCK GEMSTONES	ORGANIC GEMSTONES
DIAMOND	AGATE	AMBER
RUBY	LAPIS LAZULI	PEARL

Other gemstones are made from rocks. For example, obsidian is a shiny, black rock. It forms from quickly cooling lava flows. When the lava hardens, obsidian forms! This rock is often cut into jewelry.

OBSIDIAN JEWELRY

OBSIDIAN

LAPIS LAZULI
JEWELRY

LAPIS LAZULI

Afghanistan is the largest producer of lapis lazuli. The rock has been mined there for thousands of years.

Lapis lazuli is a beautiful blue rock. This rock forms deep below Earth's surface. Heat and pressure change other rocks into lapis lazuli. The rock has been used to make jewelry and other decorations for centuries!

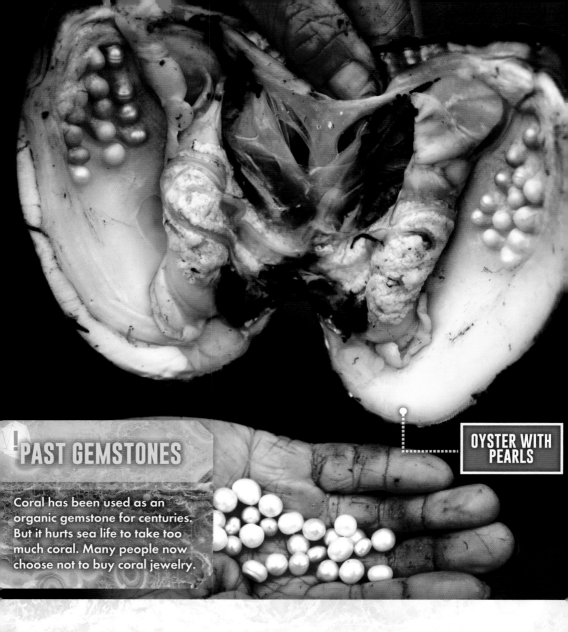

PAST GEMSTONES

Coral has been used as an organic gemstone for centuries. But it hurts sea life to take too much coral. Many people now choose not to buy coral jewelry.

OYSTER WITH PEARLS

Organic gemstones are created by living **organisms**. Pearls are popular organic gemstones. They come from oysters. When sand or other material gets stuck inside oyster shells, it is coated with **nacre**. Layers of nacre are added over many years. This forms a pearl!

Amber is another organic gemstone. Some trees give off a sticky liquid called **resin**. Resin can harden into amber. Valuable pieces of amber often contain ancient insects and plants.

HOW DO PEARLS FORM?

SAND   MANTLE   NACRE   SHELL   PEARL

1 FOREIGN MATERIAL SUCH AS SAND GETS STUCK BETWEEN THE SHELL AND MANTLE.

2 THE MANTLE LETS OUT A MATERIAL CALLED NACRE.

3 LAYERS OF NACRE BUILD AROUND THE FOREIGN OBJECT, FORMING A PEARL.

CUT AND POLISHED GARNET

UNCUT GARNET

Crystals, rocks, and organic materials look very different from finished gems. They may be rough and dull. Cutting and polishing can transform a stone. Opaque gemstones are often cut into ovals and polished. Some are carved with pictures.

Facets are cut into transparent gems. Light bounces through these sharp angles, making the gemstones sparkle. Cutting gems removes a large amount of material. Finished gems are much smaller than their original rough size!

CUTTING GARNET

Today, artificial gems are also popular. Scientists heat powdered chemicals. The chemicals melt and reform as crystals. Crystal pulling is another popular way to make gems. A machine dips a tiny crystal into very hot material. As it pulls away, crystals grow from the melted strands.

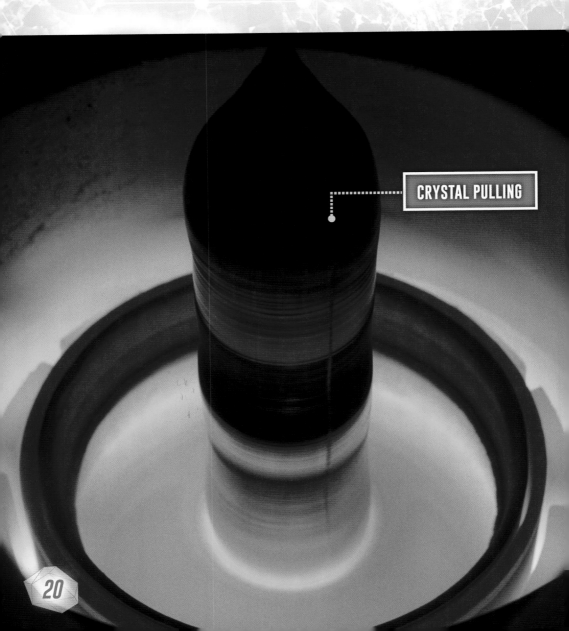

CRYSTAL PULLING

! JUST AS REAL

Human-made diamonds are grown in labs. But they are identical to diamonds found in nature!

ARTIFICIAL DIAMOND MACHINE

DIAMOND CREATION CHAMBER

Human-made diamonds are popular, too. Tiny diamonds are placed in a machine. Scientists pump gases into the machine. This makes the diamonds grow!

HOW ARE GEMSTONES USED?

Throughout human history, gemstones have been valued for their beauty. **Lapidaries** are people who work with gemstones. They use tumblers and powerful saws to give gems their best look. They cut facets to create brilliant gems!

Royals often use gems as symbols of wealth and power. The crown jewels of the United Kingdom include many famous gems. They even include one of the world's largest diamonds!

LAPIDARY CUTTING GEMSTONE

**CROWN JEWELS OF
THE UNITED KINGDOM**

THE STAR OF AFRICA

The Great Star of Africa is one of
the world's largest diamonds.
This 530-carat gemstone is one of
the United Kingdom's crown jewels.

Gems have often been used in art. **Renaissance** painters used an expensive blue paint called ultramarine. It was made from lapis lazuli powder. Gems were also used in ceremonies. The first diamond engagement ring was given in 1477!

PAINTING WITH ULTRAMARINE PAINT

DIAMOND DRILL BIT

Today, gems are valued for more than just beauty. Diamonds are the hardest natural material on Earth. Diamond-coated saws are used for cutting the toughest materials. Diamond drill bits are used to drill for natural resources. Crushed diamond is used for polishing gems and other surfaces!

DRILLING FOR NATURAL RESOURCES

SOLAR PANELS

Gems are also used in technology. For example, diamonds are used to draw heat out of electronic devices. This leads to technology that works better. Scientists have even studied diamonds to improve solar energy!

Other gemstones are useful in technology, too. Rubies are used in laser pointers and bar code scanners. Sapphires are used in cell phones and satellites. They can be used to create strong glass on armored vehicles and watch faces!

GROW YOUR OWN GEM

MATERIALS

- 1 CUP WATER
- 3 CUPS GRANULATED SUGAR
- GLASS JAR
- PENCIL
- STRING
- FOOD COLORING (OPTIONAL)

SUGAR CRYSTAL

DIRECTIONS

1. With an adult, boil 1 cup of water.

2. Add 3 cups of sugar to the water. Stir it in.

3. Pour the solution into a glass jar. Add a few drops of food coloring if desired.

4. Tie the string to the pencil. Place the pencil over the jar so the string is submerged in the solution.

5. Watch sugar crystals grow! They will get larger over several days.

6. Try making your own gemstone by cutting the crystals into a new shape.

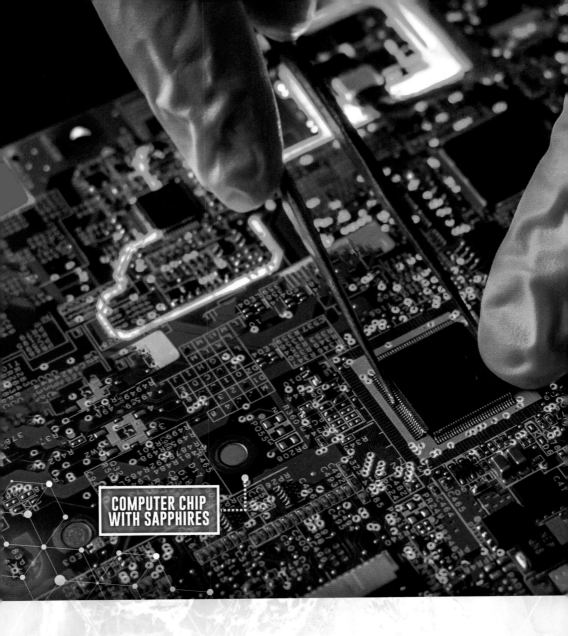

COMPUTER CHIP
WITH SAPPHIRES

Gemstones have long been used to create beautiful art
and jewelry. Their beauty has excited people for centuries.
Today, their use in technology is just as exciting!

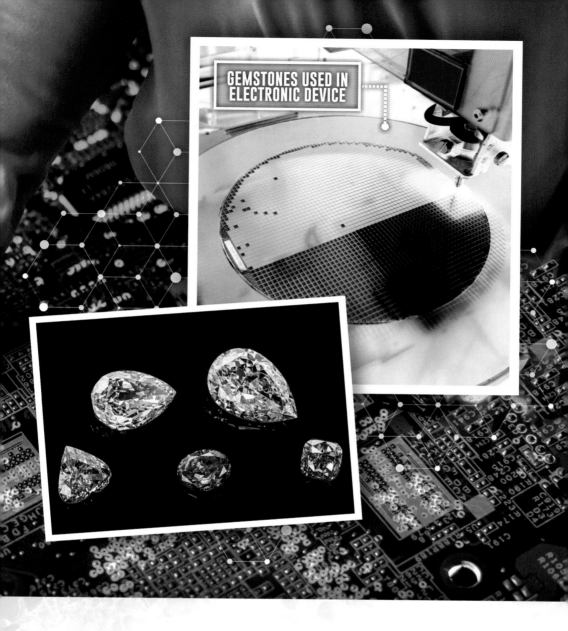

GEMSTONES USED IN ELECTRONIC DEVICE

In the future, people will likely continue using gemstones in art and technology. Jewelers will make more beautiful jewelry. Scientists will find ways to improve today's tools. They might even discover new uses for gemstones. Gemstones may help build the computers of the future!

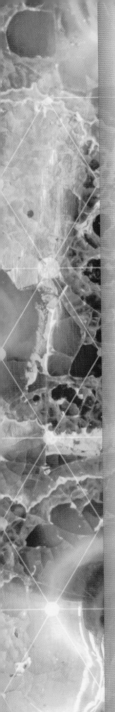

GLOSSARY

artificial—created by humans or machines

crystal pulling—a process for growing crystals by lifting them from very hot material

crystals—solid materials whose atoms are arranged in specific patterns; atoms are the smallest part of a material that can exist.

dissolved—mixed into a solution such as water

embedded—firmly inserted inside of something

facets—the flat sides of a cut gemstone

lapidaries—people who polish or cut gemstones

luster—the way a gemstone looks in reflected light

minerals—materials that make up crystals

Mohs scale—a scale that measures the hardness of rocks

nacre—a shiny coating made by clams and oysters to protect themselves from sand and other harmful intruders

natural resources—materials that are found in nature

opaque—blocking light

organic—made from living organisms

organisms—living things

Renaissance—a period of growth in arts and writing during the 1300s to 1600s in Europe

resin—a sticky liquid given off by some trees; insects are often fossilized in resin.

translucent—allowing some light to pass through

transparent—the quality of allowing light to pass through

TO LEARN MORE

AT THE LIBRARY

Callery, Sean, and Miranda Smith. *Rocks, Minerals, & Gems.* New York, N.Y.: Scholastic, 2016.

Parish, Patrick. *Crystals.* Minneapolis, Minn.: Bellwether Media, 2020.

Romaine, Garret. *Geology Lab for Kids.* Beverly, Mass.: Quarry Books, 2017.

ON THE WEB

FACTSURFER

Factsurfer.com gives you a safe, fun way to find more information.

1. Go to www.factsurfer.com.

2. Enter "gemstones" into the search box and click Q.

3. Select your book cover to see a list of related web sites.

LABRADORITE

31

INDEX